MARTINI WISDOM

And other midlife
musings from
The Three Tomatoes

Cheryl Benton and Roni Jenkins

Cover Photo iStock and interior images iStock and Shutterstock.

Visit our website at www.thethreetomatoes.com

Printed in the United States of America

First Printing: November 2018
The Three Tomatoes Publishing

ISBN: 978-0-578-41014-2

Dedication

This book is dedicated to all the fun loving and free-spirited women we know who are fully enjoying life at every age and every stage.

"I like to have a martini,

two at the very most.

After three I'm under the table, After

four I'm under my host."

— Dororthy Parker

We enjoy the occasional martini and are mindful of the quote attributed to Dorothy Parker. Though some question if Ms. Parker actually ever said this, we say screw the skeptics, and three cheers to Dorothy.

There's definitely something to be said for viewing midlife and beyond through a martini glass. Our "martini ladies" have been spouting their wisdom - sometimes borrowed, sometimes new - once a week in The Three Tomatoes newsletters for quite some time. Our smart, savvy readers like their irreverent view of life. We hope you will too. Feel free to share with your BFFs.

Cheers,

Cheryl Benton and Roni Jenkins
www.thethreetomatoes.com

Martini Wisdom from The Three Tomatoes

Darlings,

When you get to be "a certain age"

being invisible is not a superpower.

You're just being ignored.

Martini Wisdom from The Three Tomatoes

Darlings,

I really don't need your approval.

That's for insecure people.

Martini Wisdom from The Three Tomatoes

Darlings,

Life is not a fairy tale. If you lose your shoe at
midnight you're drunk.

Martini Wisdom from The Three Tomatoes

Darlings,

Pick a man who will ruin your lipstick,

not your mascara.

Martini Wisdom from The Three Tomatoes

Darlings,

Age and treachery will always overcome

youth and skill.

Martini Wisdom from The Three Tomatoes

Darling Brain,

Can we please sleep tonight instead of recounting every stupid decision I've ever made? Thank you from the rest of my body.

Martini Wisdom from The Three Tomatoes

Darlings,

Shenanigans. If you don't know how to spell

it, you've never lived it.

Martini Wisdom from The Three Tomatoes

Darlings,

Embrace the glutens and GMO's.

Remember, the vodka will kill the wheat.

Martini Wisdom from The Three Tomatoes

Darlings,

I'm at the age where I just say what I think
and then watch the chaos ensue.

Martini Wisdom from The Three Tomatoes

Darlings,

There are two kinds of shopping companions.
The ones who say "buy it" are called BFFs.
The ones who say "you don't need that" are
called husbands.

Martini Wisdom from The Three Tomatoes

Darlings,

"Why do you need so many shoes?"

said no woman ever.

Martini Wisdom from The Three Tomatoes

Darlings,

I can't make everyone happy.

I'm not bacon!

Martini Wisdom from The Three Tomatoes

Darlings,

We'll always be best friends.

You know way too much about me.

Martini Wisdom from The Three Tomatoes

Darlings,

I do yoga to relieve stress...just kidding.

I drink wine in yoga pants.

Martini Wisdom from The Three Tomatoes

Darlings,

I may be crazy, but all the best people are,

don't you think?

Martini Wisdom from The Three Tomatoes

Darlings,

When he tells you it's not hot in here, it's just you, don't you want to put his penis in that mammogram machine and squeeze?

Martini Wisdom from The Three Tomatoes

Darlings,

I hate it when I don't forward a chain letter

and I die the next day.

Martini Wisdom from The Three Tomatoes

Dear Diet,

I'm breaking up with you. It's not you it's me. You are boring, bland, and I can't stop cheating on you. Let's try again next year.

Martini Wisdom from The Three Tomatoes

Darlings,

Cinderella is proof that a new pair of shoes

can change your life.

Martini Wisdom from The Three Tomatoes

Darlings,

Not to brag or anything, but I can still fit into
the earrings I wore in high school.

Martini Wisdom from The Three Tomatoes

Darlings,

The bigger your handbag the smaller your
ass looks.

Martini Wisdom from The Three Tomatoes

Darlings,

10 reps lifting your martini glass might tone your arms, but by then you won't care.

Martini Wisdom from The Three Tomatoes

Darlings,

BFFs don't care if your house is clean.

They care if you have wine and chocolate.

Martini Wisdom from The Three Tomatoes

Dear Karma,

I have a list of people you missed.

Martini Wisdom from The Three Tomatoes

Darlings,

In my defense, it was after midnight

and we had polished off two bottles of wine.

Martini Wisdom from The Three Tomatoes

Darlings,

Of course, money doesn't buy you happiness,

but wouldn't you rather cry in a mansion?

Martini Wisdom from The Three Tomatoes

Darlings,

Warning: Real life may appear less perfect

than Facebook life.

Martini Wisdom from The Three Tomatoes

Darlings,

When Jane told Dick she had nothing to wear,

he said she had a closet full of clothes.

There's a reason he's called Dick.

Martini Wisdom from The Three Tomatoes

Darlings,

Cinderella and Prince Charming did not live happily ever after. Moral: If the shoe fits you don't have to wear it.

Martini Wisdom from The Three Tomatoes

Darlings,

I prefer to meet men the old-fashioned way
- through alcohol and poor judgement.

Martini Wisdom from The Three Tomatoes

Darlings,

Today I will live in the moment. Unless it's unpleasant and then I will drink wine.

Martini Wisdom from The Three Tomatoes

Darlings,

If cauliflower can be pizza, you can be whatever the hell you want to be.

Martini Wisdom from The Three Tomatoes

Darlings,

Life is like underwear.

Change is good.

Martini Wisdom from The Three Tomatoes

Darlings,

How are mothers and martinis alike?

The older you get

the more you appreciate them.

Martini Wisdom from The Three Tomatoes

Darlings,

How many countless hours have you spent

worrying about things that never happened?

That's what I thought.

Martini Wisdom from The Three Tomatoes

Darlings,

The world is your oyster. Just make sure to chug it down with a shot of vodka.

Martini Wisdom from The Three Tomatoes

Darlings,

Those of you who write "u" instead of "you" and "k" instead of "okay," what do you do with all your spare time?

Martini Wisdom from The Three Tomatoes

Darlings,

I saw a man alone at Starbucks, just drinking coffee, with no digital device in his hand. He must be a psycho.

Martini Wisdom from The Three Tomatoes

Darlings,

When life shuts a door...open it again.

That's how they work.

Martini Wisdom from The Three Tomatoes

January 4...

Dear New Year's Resolutions,

It was fun while it lasted.

Martini Wisdom from The Three Tomatoes

Darlings,

Online stalking is all fun and games until

you accidentally hit the like button.

Martini Wisdom from The Three Tomatoes

Dear Santa,

I was naughty, and it was so worth it.

Martini Wisdom from The Three Tomatoes

Darlings,

When life gives you lemons, make a martini.

Martini Wisdom from The Three Tomatoes

Darlings,

Keep smiling. It will make people

wonder what you're up to.

Martini Wisdom from The Three Tomatoes

Darlings,

I make wine disappear.

What's your superpower?

Martini Wisdom from The Three Tomatoes

Darlings,

My heart says chocolate, but my jeans say,

"Good Lord woman eat a salad."

Martini Wisdom from The Three Tomatoes

Darlings,

It's the little things that count – like when your friend refills your wine glass without being asked.

Martini Wisdom from The Three Tomatoes

Darlings,

When it comes to RSVPs, a simple yes or no will suffice. Maybe is not an option.

Martini Wisdom from The Three Tomatoes

Darlings,

The road is full of flat squirrels who couldn't make a decision. Don't be a squirrel.

Martini Wisdom from The Three Tomatoes

Darlings,

Wouldn't it be nice if we all remembered what we learned in kindergarten? Be nice to everyone, share, and try not to pee in your pants.

About Us

From the publishers of The Three Tomatoes, a digital lifestyle magazine for women, *Martini Wisdom* is the perfect anecdote to all those motivational and inspirational books about midlife and beyond. It's the inappropriate thought bubbles that the "martini ladies" dare to say out loud. Come on...you know you've had some of these thoughts too. It's the perfect anywhere read and you're going to want to share it with your BFFs too.

The Three Tomatoes mother and daughter duo, Cheryl Benton and Roni Jenkins, are the tomatoes behind Martini Wisdom. Visit us at The Three Tomatoes, www.thethreetomatoes.com

PS: If you like the book, please leave a review on Amazon.

97080805R00033

Made in the USA
San Bernardino, CA
21 November 2018